SMALL STEPS TO SAVE THE WORLD

JOIN THE SMALL STEPS REVOLUTION TODAY

USING WATER WISELY

BY ROBIN TWIDDY

Enslow PUBLISHING

Published in 2023 by Enslow Publishing, LLC
29 East 21st Street, New York, NY 10010

This edition is published by arrangement with Booklife Publishing

Edited by:
Madeline Tyler

Designed by:
Drue Rintoul

Cataloging-in-Publication Data

Names: Twiddy, Robin.
Title: Using water wisely / Robin Twiddy.
Description: New York : Enslow Publishing, 2023. | Series: Small steps to save the world | Includes glossary and index.
Identifiers: ISBN 9781978530461 (pbk.) | ISBN 9781978530485 (library bound) | ISBN 9781978530478 (6 pack) | ISBN 9781978530492 (ebook)
Subjects: LCSH: Water conservation--Juvenile literature. | Water-supply--Juvenile literature. | Water quality--Juvenile literature.
Classification: LCC TD348.T954 2023 | DDC 333.79'16--dc23

Manufactured in the United States of America

CPSIA compliance information: Batch #CSENS23: For further information contact Enslow Publishing LLC, New York, New York at 1-800-398-2504

Please visit our website, www.enslowpublishing.com. For a free color catalog of all our high-quality books, call toll free 1-800-398-2504 or fax 1-877-980-4454.

Find us on

PHOTO CREDITS

Images are courtesy of Shutterstock.com. With thanks to Getty Images, Thinkstock Photo and iStockphoto. 4&5 – Prostock-studio, seeshooteatrepeat, Hung Chung Chih, WvdMPhotography, chromatos, Rich Carey, MelnikovSergei. 6&7 – Midstream. 8&9 – Prostock-studio, Glenn R. Specht-grs photo, DenisProduction.com. 10&11 – zombiu26, NavinTar, Prostock-studio. 12&13 – GreenCam1, LedyX, OlegDoroshin, Paul Maguire, urbanbuzz, Kekyalyaynen, Vastram, Infinity T29, arhendrix, Avatar_023, ThomBal, victoras, GreenCam1, Prostock-studio. 14&15 – Prostock-studio, Richard Pratt, wavebreakmedia, DenisProduction.com, Grigvovan. 16&17 – Maridav, Prostock-studio, somrak jendee. 18&19 – DGLimages, Volurol, Casezy idea, Monkey Business Images, Diego Cervo, Prostock-studio. 20&21 – Asier Romero, Prostock-studio, goodmoments, gornostay, Lucian Coman, MexChriss, DJTaylor. 22&23 – Prostock-studio, 24K-Production, Aleksandr Ozerov, Kodda. 24&25 – Prostock-studio, kamilpetran, Oliver Hoffmann. 26&27 – Prostock-studio, Lopolo, Prostock-studio, Brocreative. 28&29 – wavebreakmedia, Igor Pushkarev. 30 – Prostock-studio.

CONTENTS

Words that look like <u>this</u> are explained in the glossary on page 31.

You can (help) Save the World

The world is in trouble and it needs your help! It needs everyone's help. No one can save the world on their own, but together we can make a change. Our planet is facing many challenges, and lots of these are because of humans. The climate crisis is a big problem. We can see how humans have made it worse by looking at changes in the weather, the oceans, and the air we breathe.

THE SMALL STEPS REVOLUTIONARIES

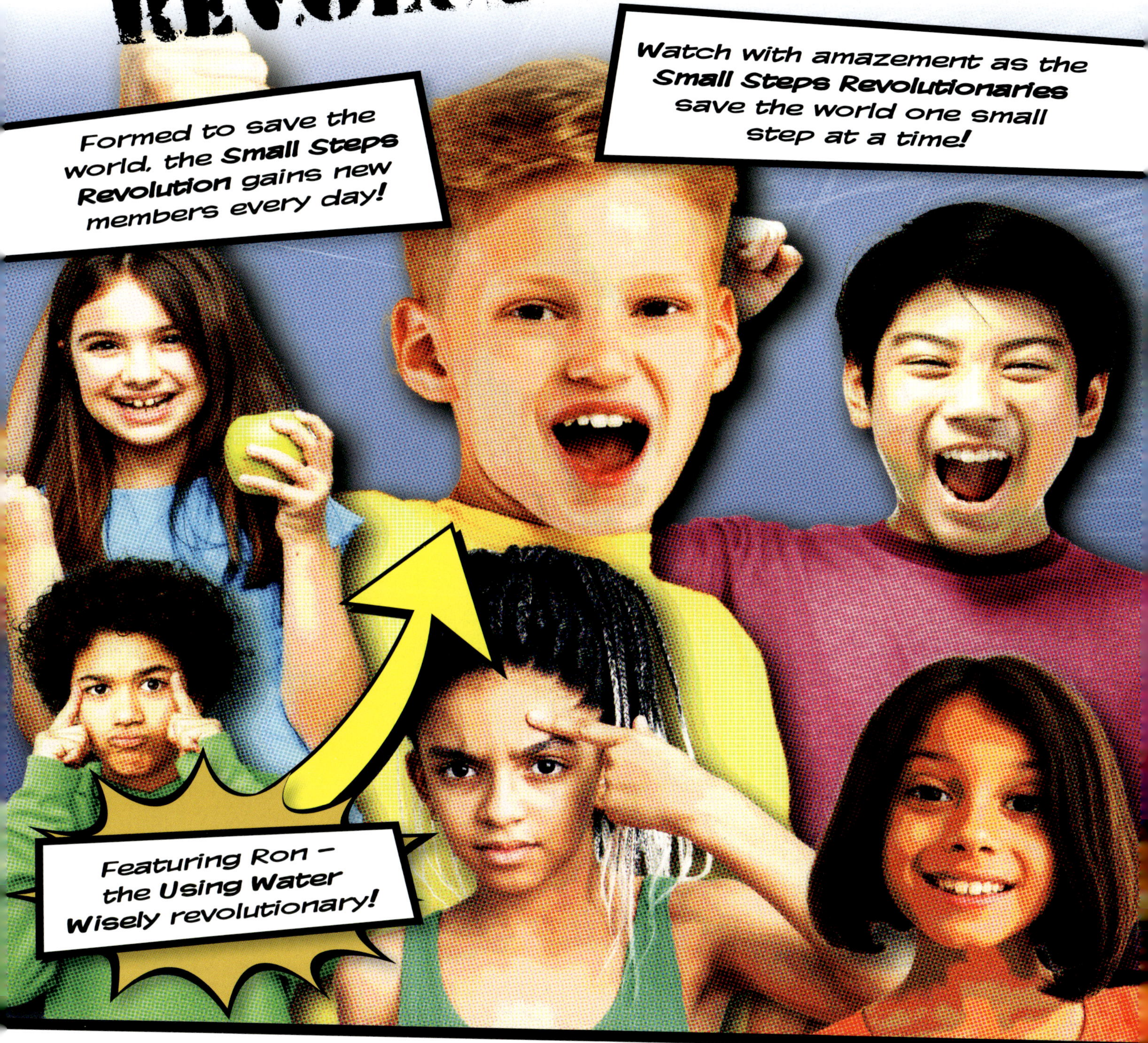

These are the Small Steps Revolutionaries. They are changing the world one step at a time. Whether it's being energy efficient or learning how to compost, eating locally or living zero waste, recycling or using water wisely, no problem is too big or too small for this band of heroes. By the time you finish this book, you too will be a member of the Small Steps Revolution. Strap in – it's time to save the world!

Grow Your Knowledge

The first step to becoming a Small Steps Revolutionary is growing your knowledge. This means learning as much as you can about the change you want to see. There are lots of ways to grow your knowledge. Here are some places to get started.

Learn from others – do you know anyone who is wise with water? Ask them about it.

Visit the library – ask the librarian to help you find books about the environment.

"Knowledge is power – arm yourself!"

"Not everything that is faced can be changed, but nothing can be changed until it is faced."
– Lucille Ball

Lucille Ball was an actor, producer, and comedian. She was very successful and made a lot of things possible for women today.

"Those who do not learn from history are doomed to repeat it!"

Thomas Kuhn was an American philosopher. He thought a lot about what we know about the world, and how we know it.

"The answers you get depend upon the questions you ask."
– Thomas Kuhn

Research online – there are lots of great websites about how to conserve water.

Ask your adult how much water you use in your household.

Use an online carbon dioxide (CO_2) calculator to find out what your carbon footprint is. (Find out more about your carbon footprint on page 24.)

SMALL STEP: GROW YOUR KNOWLEDGE!

Knowledge is important, but make sure that the information you look at is accurate. A good way to do that is to see who else agrees, writes, or talks about the same information. Has it come from a reliable place or person?

Getting Wise About Water

Ron is a Small Steps Revolutionary. Being a Small Steps Revolutionary means making small changes in your own life to help make a change around the world and inspire others to do the same.

It can be hard to think about how the small things we do have an effect on the world, but they do. It is up to us to decide what that effect will be. As a Small Steps Revolutionary, you will learn how to make positive choices and help others to do the same.

Before we get into how to be wiser with water, we are going to need to know a bit more about the water in our lives.

Where Does My Water Come From?

THE WATER CYCLE

Earth's water is used and reused again and again. It goes around in a cycle, so we call it the water cycle.

1 **Water evaporates** – this means the sun warms it up until it turns into water vapor and rises up in the air.

2 **Water condenses** – this means the water vapor cools down enough to turn into clouds.

3 **Rain and snow** – when the cloud is heavy enough, it falls back down as rain or snow.

4 **Back to the sea** – the water collects in lakes and rivers and is taken back to the sea or the ocean, where the cycle begins again.

WHERE DOES TAP WATER COME FROM?

Water is collected from rivers, lakes, and underground reservoirs. It then goes to buildings that clean the water and make it safe to drink. It is often stored in huge tanks, ready to be sent to our homes by pipes. Bottled water comes from the same places as tap water.

Safe chemicals are also added to tap water to kill germs. If this did not happen, people might get ill.

These machines are cleaning the water.

Where Does It Come From, Where Does It Go?

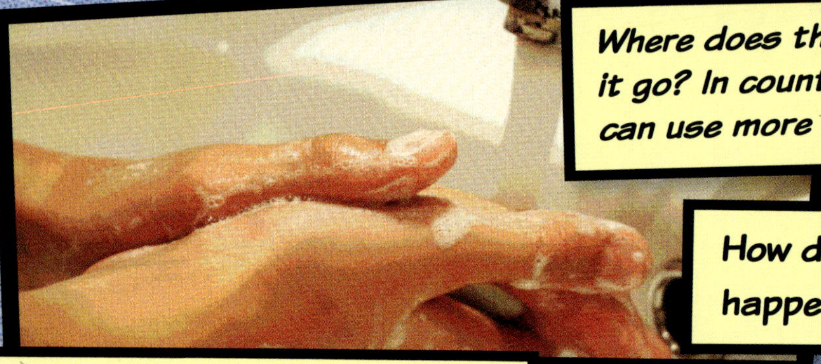

Where does the water come from and where does it go? In countries with running water, each person can use more than 250 gallons (946 L) every day.

How does water get to our taps, and what happens when it runs down the drain?

When Carmine runs this tap, the water runs down the drain. And then where?

The water rushes through the plumbing of her home...

... and moves through underground pipes called the sewage system.

Eventually the water makes it to a treatment plant. Here, all the things that shouldn't be in the water are taken out.

The water is cleaned several times, then...

... the clean water is returned to rivers, lakes, and reservoirs.

Water is pumped from rivers, lakes, and reservoirs.
It travels to a treatment plant where it is cleaned several times.
The water is chlorinated, which means a chemical is added that kills harmful things that might be in the water.
The treated water is pumped into a network of pipes that run underground.
The pipes lead to the plumbing in your house...
... and back to your taps!
Wow, the cycle never ends!

Think Before You Pour Down the Sink!

Stop! Don't pour that water down the sink. The less water we pour down the sink, the better. There are lots of ways we can reuse old water instead of wasting new water. Here are some ways in which you can reuse water and save the planet.

We can collect rainwater and reuse it for all sorts of things, such as washing the car or windows. If you want to learn more about saving rainwater, my friend Brenda has some great water-saving tips on page 20!

Water that has been used in the house is called gray water.

Don't get rid of your dishwashing water. Give it to your plants instead.

Top Tip: Before you wash your plates, scrape all the food off so there isn't any left in the dishwashing water.

Water used to boil pasta or wash vegetables can be used to water indoor plants.

SMALL STEP: REUSE WATER FROM COOKING AND WASHING AND GIVE IT TO YOUR GARDEN OR INDOOR PLANTS

When you shower, collect the water in buckets. You can sprinkle this water over the lawn.

What If I Use Too Much Water?

Just under three-quarters of Earth is covered in water. That might sound like a lot, but we cannot drink most of it. This is because water from the ocean is too salty, and we can only drink fresh water. But some of the fresh water is frozen in glaciers, deep in the soil, or underground so we can't get it. The rest of it comes from rivers and lakes, and this is the fresh water we can drink.

If humans don't use water wisely, it means the rivers and lakes will be drained of their water before it can be recycled. Many animals and plants need big rivers and lakes to survive. Using too much water will destroy their homes.

Wasting water can lead to dried-up rivers.

SMALL STEP:
ASK YOURSELF IF YOU REALLY NEED TO USE THE WATER

Small Steps to Save Water

Being a Small Steps Revolutionary is all about the small things we do – making small changes in our lives that add up to big changes in the world. We just have to make sure that we can stick to these changes.

Make sure that you don't leave the tap running when you are brushing your teeth.

Try putting on your favorite song when you use the shower. See if you can finish showering before the song finishes. It is easy to lose track of time in the shower, and this is a fun way to make sure that your showers are short.

Ron has some more tips for using water wisely around the house.

Using the same cup all day for drinks can save water on washing up. You can do the same with plates if they're not too dirty.

If you use a dishwasher, you can save water by getting good at filling the machine. Turn it into a puzzle to see how much you can fit in.

Keep a bottle of water in the fridge. That way you can save on water by getting a cold drink from the fridge instead of running the tap until it is cold!

SMALL STEPS:

- MAKE SAVING WATER AT HOME FUN
- DON'T LEAVE TAPS RUNNING
- KEEP SHOWERS SHORT
- REUSE CUPS AND PLATES UNTIL THEY NEED TO BE CLEANED
- KEEP WATER IN THE FRIDGE

Remember – the Small Steps become easier the more you do them!

Water in the Garden

We've made lots of **Small Steps** toward using water wisely, but for this next one we need some help. This is Brenda, and she's a **Small Steps Revolutionary** just like me. She is an expert in the **Small Steps** you can take in the garden!

Thanks, Ron. We can change the world in so many ways, even from our own gardens. Lots of people use fresh water in their gardens to water their plants, and saving water in the garden is just as important as saving water in your home.

There are lots of things we can do to save water in the garden. Let me show you a few **Small Steps** you can take today.

Garden hoses can use over 250 gallons (946 L) of water in one hour! Swap the garden hose for a watering can instead – these use much less water.

Sprinklers use way too much water – you should avoid using them if you can.

If you can, add a rain barrel to your garden. A rain barrel is a container that catches rainwater.

When you fill up your watering can, you can use the rainwater from the rain barrel instead of fresh water from the tap or a hose!

SMALL STEPS:

- WATER PLANTS WITH A WATERING CAN INSTEAD OF A HOSE
- SAVE AND USE RAINWATER

Water Around the World

Our planet is home to over 7 billion people – that's a lot of people, and that number is always going up. The amount of water on our planet never really changes. This means that the same amount of water needs to be shared by more and more people.

There are many ways that we are making it harder to get water. Some of these ways may not be very easy to see right away. When we travel by car, bus, or plane, we are burning fossil fuels to power them. When we use the TV, computers, and even the lights in our homes, we are using power that is often made by burning fossil fuels. This all adds to the amount of CO_2 in the atmosphere and adds to the climate crisis.

Climate crisis is the name for the serious problems caused by changes to the world's weather. These problems happen because humans burn fossil fuels, which means the planet's temperature rises in many areas. This can cause droughts.

Droughts are a big problem because we need to drink water to stay alive. We also need water for cleaning and for growing food.

SMALL STEP: THINK GLOBALLY – KEEP IN MIND THAT THE SMALL THINGS WE DO HAVE BIG IMPACTS

Water and Your Carbon Footprint

What is a carbon footprint? It is the amount of CO_2 that you make through the things you do. You can find information online to help you get a good idea about what your carbon footprint is like.

Even running the tap can add to your carbon footprint. The pumps that push the water through the pipes to your house use energy – this energy is often made by burning fossil fuels and is adding to your carbon footprint.

A good **Small Steps Revolutionary** does their best to have the smallest carbon footprint they can. To learn about other ways to lower your carbon footprint and take some **Small Steps** toward saving the world, check out the books from the other revolutionaries – they will help get you started, but the rest is up to you!

Becoming a Champion of Change

Being a Small Steps Revolutionary is more than just taking Small Steps yourself – it also means being a champion of change. We can do this by showing others the steps we are taking and sharing our passion for using water wisely.

RAISING AWARENESS

There are lots of ways that you can raise awareness as a Small Steps Revolutionary. Some revolutionaries use social media to share their message. Recruit an adult to help you manage an account. Remember not to use social media without an adult you trust.

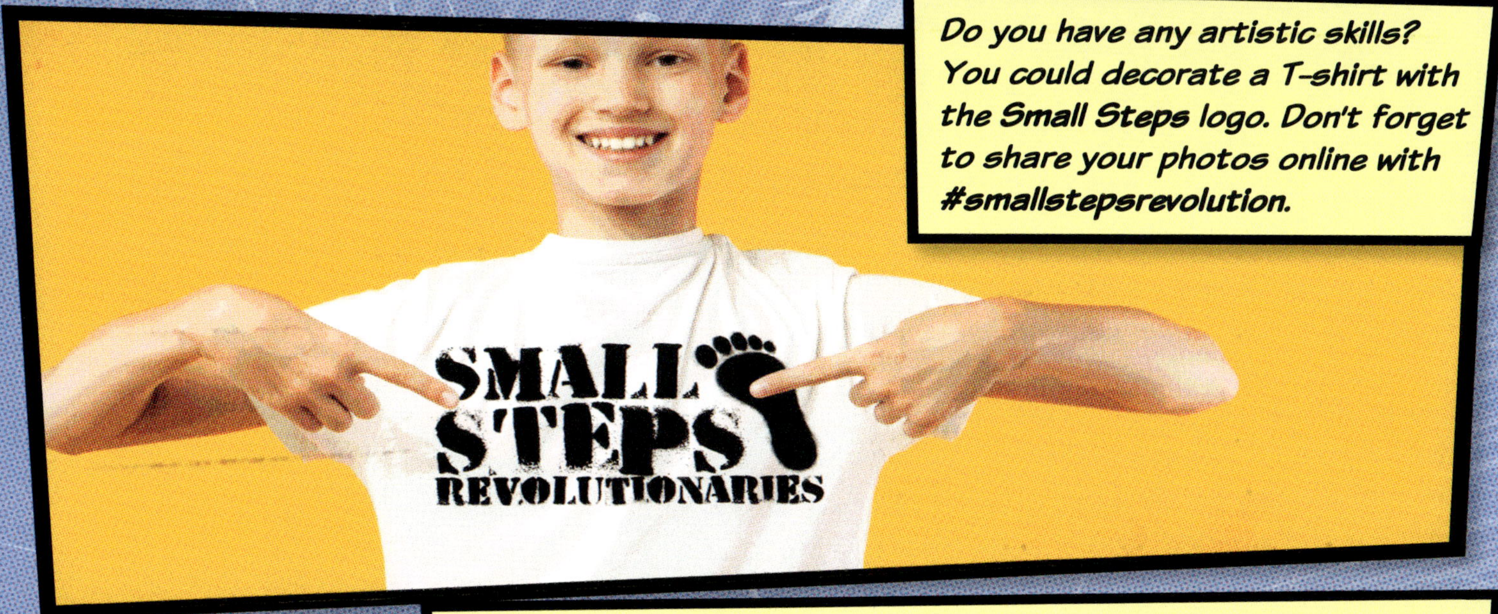

Remember, some people might not have met anyone making the changes you are making, so be nice when you talk about using water wisely with them. People are more likely to try to make a change themselves if you are helpful instead of being mean to them – this is the **Small Steps** way!

SMALL STEPS: SPREAD THE MESSAGE

Ethical Living

Using water wisely is only one part of the Small Steps Revolution, so what does it mean to be a Small Steps Revolutionary? It means living ethically – living the best life you can. To live ethically, you need to think about the effect your actions have on the world around you.

Being wise with water all the time is not easy and won't happen overnight. Remember the golden rule: Small Steps Lead to Big Change. Focus on making small changes that you can keep to every day. Every small step you take will bring you closer to using water wisely.

THE FIVE Rs

A good way to guide your actions as a Small Steps Revolutionary is to live by the Five Rs. They are:

REFUSE – BEFORE YOU BUY SOMETHING, THINK HARD ABOUT WHETHER YOU NEED IT OR NOT. IF YOU DON'T, THEN REFUSE TO BUY OR ACCEPT IT.

REDUCE – SOME THINGS YOU WILL NOT BE ABLE TO REFUSE, BUT YOU CAN USE LESS. THIS WILL MEAN YOU CREATE LESS WASTE.

REUSE – BEFORE YOU THROW SOMETHING AWAY, THINK ABOUT WHETHER THAT THING CAN BE USED AGAIN. ONLY REPLACE SOMETHING IF IT CAN'T BE USED AGAIN.

REPURPOSE – THIS IS ANOTHER WAY OF SAYING UPCYCLE. IF YOU CAN, FIND A NEW WAY TO USE SOMETHING INSTEAD OF THROWING IT AWAY.

RECYCLE – IF YOU CAN'T DO ANY OF THESE THINGS, THEN YOU SHOULD TRY TO RECYCLE. MAKE SURE THAT WHAT YOU PUT INTO YOUR RECYCLING BIN CAN BE RECYCLED BY YOUR LOCAL RECYCLING CENTER.

Manifesto

THE USING WATER WISELY MANIFESTO

- GROW YOUR KNOWLEDGE
- REUSE WATER FROM COOKING AND WASHING AND GIVE IT TO YOUR GARDEN OR INDOOR PLANTS
- ASK YOURSELF IF YOU REALLY NEED TO USE THE WATER
- MAKE SAVING WATER AT HOME FUN
- DON'T LEAVE TAPS RUNNING
- KEEP SHOWERS SHORT
- REUSE CUPS AND PLATES UNTIL THEY NEED TO BE CLEANED
- KEEP WATER IN THE FRIDGE
- WATER PLANTS WITH A WATERING CAN INSTEAD OF A HOSE
- SAVE AND USE RAINWATER
- KEEP IN MIND THAT THE SMALL THINGS WE DO HAVE BIG IMPACTS
- LEARN ABOUT YOUR CARBON FOOTPRINT
- SPREAD THE MESSAGE

You are now a full member of the **Small Steps Revolution.** Keep on taking small, sustainable steps, spreading the word, and inspiring others to do the same. Together we can and will **Save the World!**

Glossary

BILLION one thousand million

CARBON DIOXIDE a natural gas that is found in the air that humans breathe out

CHEMICALS substances that materials are made from

CLIMATE CRISIS serious problems being caused by changes to the world's weather, caused by humans and the release of greenhouse gases into the environment

CONSERVE to keep something from running out or disappearing

CYCLE something that goes around

DROUGHTS times with very little rain that can lead to a lack of water

ENCOURAGE to say good things to help someone do something

ENVIRONMENT all the things that make up the natural world

FOSSIL FUELS things such as coal and oil that are made naturally over billions of years and burned to make energy

GLACIERS big, slow-moving rivers of ice

PHILOSOPHER a person who thinks about the world and what it means to be human

PRODUCER someone who pays for and works on TV programs and films

RECRUIT to bring a member into a group

RELIABLE can be trusted

RESERVOIRS places where things are stored for future use

RESPONSIBILITY a need for someone to do something

RUNNING WATER water that goes in and out of homes through pipes

SUSTAINABLE able to be used without damaging future generations

Index